A Series of Poems

PALMETTO
PUBLISHING
Charleston, SC
www.PalmettoPublishing.com

Copyright © 2024 by Mariam Shams Tabrez

All rights reserved
No portion of this book may be reproduced, stored in a retrieval system, or transmitted in any form by any means-electronic, mechanical, photocopy, recording, or other-except for brief quotations in printed reviews, without prior permission of the author.

Hardcover ISBN: 979-8-8229-4301-8
Paperback ISBN: 979-8-8229-4302-5
eBook ISBN: 979-8-8229-4303-2

Scattered
A Series of Poems

Mariam Shams Tabrez

Dedication

I want to dedicate this poetry book to my loving and inspiring parents, Dr. Shams and Dr. Salma Tabrez, and my beautiful and smart (feels odd to be this sincere with you both lol) sisters Elsa and Sana.

Thank you Aboo for reading Rumi, Iqbal, and many other great poets to us since we were young and for being an incredible poet yourself.

Thank you Amma for also being an incredible poet and a true inspiration to me as a mother, sister, daughter, wife, friend, and physician.

Thank you Appa and Sana for always supporting me through my sad girl moments.

This poetry book is a compilation of all of my thoughts, feelings, and experiences from when I was 17 all the way up to 27.

I believe poetry was never meant to be linear, calculated, or themed.

I believe poetry is expressive, dynamic, unique, and *scattered*.

Hopefully you enjoy and maybe resonate with these musings.

Love, Mariam

1.

Tonight, for the first time, I watched the blue sky fall
asleep
It was slow, it was glorious, and it was deep
As the colors shifted and the clouds danced to the beat
of the wind in hues of orange and red
The moon was gracing us with her creases and
crevices, the sun had quickly fled
He knew this slumber was bigger than him
So he escaped and the light in his eyes became dim
So as I watched the blue sky fall asleep, I was
wondering if you did the same
If you knew for the darkness, the moon was never to
blame
This was nature's course and every light fades
As she rises in the darkness and the tears cascade.

2.

You feel like an imposter everywhere you go
Not quite belonging anywhere
You were raised to live in a world much different than this one
No one told you it would be this difficult
No one taught you your worth
No one told you self love was a matter of survival
Now you lay here unsure of yourself when all I see is potential and beauty.

3.

I guess by setting you free I'm waiting for something to happen
For the ground to break, for the sky to open, for the dry desert to dampen
All the impossible seemed possible in your eyes
The fear, the angst, would fade out, as if disguised
But you went in another direction, lowering your gaze
Left me speechless, crestfallen, caught in a daze
Because I didn't think this was temporary, some sort of mirage
Bu I also didn't think my feelings would grow, so hard for me to dodge
The thought of losing you to another is just too hard to bear
The thought of you leaning on another just seems so unfair
To me as a well-wisher and an accomplice of love
But now I'm here in silence, with nowhere to look except above.

4.

Climbing up a mountain
In search of your embrace
I use the moon as an excuse to look up at your face
Your presence, your aura is something of a view
So high up off the ground only if you knew
The dedication, the strength it took to reach to your level
To push away all the odds, to trick the conniving devil
Into believing that your lust was something of holy fire
A mere need for fulfillment, the purest desire
That a poor lover feels when residing near the ground
That a poor lover yields when being coercively drowned
A force that pushes me away too soon
A force that suppresses my precious view of the moon.

5.

The art of knowing is a strange notion
Gaining information, setting our intellectual journeys in motion
But why do we know what we know?
Why are we able to see the world around us and not be fully consumed by its complexity?
Pages of school textbooks are read daily, yet we are not engrossed by their density
We are taught that reading is necessary and necessary is a good GPA, and a good GPA is our ticket to the big time
Memorize the right information and up the social ladder we'll climb
With no recollection of the marvels we were so lucky to be exposed to
The world's abstractions we should know merely become something we once knew.

6.

Since the day I was born to the days following after
You were the first one to hold me up and leave me with laughter
Taking care of our family, protecting our feelings
You taught me there's more to your work than a physician's healing
A physician cures the body while the doctor cures the soul
When I was left hopeless on the ground you made me feel whole
You kept telling me, "Dream Big, Work Hard, Be Honest, my dear"
Approach life with no hesitation, absolutely no fear
Because our Creator has a master plan, in it you should trust
Designed us from nothing, created us from dust
Though this world may seem daunting, every step a trial
I know you will always provide me with wise words and a sincere big smile.
I love you, Aboo. The best father anyone could ask for.

7.

He came into my life, he came to me
So quick, so fast I forgot to breathe
He left me, he left me for the beautiful sky
He told me, he told me I won't say goodbye
Because you're too pretty, this is my city, and the moonlight brings out your eyes.

8.

Anger is a strange thing
It can engulf the soul so sudden so quick
Like a raging fire starting from a candle's one single wick
It's a force that stops for no one and affects everyone
It doesn't cease to diminish until the damage is done
Because words once spoken and a flame once sparked are quite similar in composition
Once they've caused their destruction there's no choice but submission.

9.

She was a blooming flower in the sun, never needing anyone
Until one day she saw a pair of daffodils billowing in unison and thought "that could be fun"
She called on the birds, the bees, and the trees to plant her a lover.

10.

It took me too long to stop forgiving you
I still loved you even after all you put me through
It took me too long to understand your game
You kept playing me leaving only myself to blame
It took too long to realize that this wasn't love you were giving me
I kept telling myself you were too scared to show how much you cared
It took me too long to forget about your beautiful eyes and unforgettable smile
Because they haunted me, lead me astray and deeper into your arms
It took me too long to stop letting you know how my day went
But it didn't take you too long to forget what we had and all the time we spent
Loving each other, completely in sync
Leaving me here breathless, leaving my heart to sink.

11.

This is for the girl who was told she couldn't do it
For the girl who was told she should just quit
Because it's a man's world and a woman is second place
Yeah, she deserves some rights but please cover her face
Because a man gets distracted and how he acted with her is now given viable excuses
The way she dresses is the cause for all the blood and the bruises
It's not his fault, he's only human, he just couldn't help himself
Well, forgive me when I tell you that this isn't just a man's world but the world of every living thing residing in it
Sorry for being so forward, like him, I'm only human, I just couldn't help myself.

12.

When you just think you're not good enough
When you forget that you're a diamond in the rough
Strong, powerful, beautiful and filled with endless wealth
When you overlook blessings such as a family and good health
Thinking that you have it bad that the world is crumbling in front of you
Forgetting that it's not about all the pain but it's about how much you grew
Because there are people in the world that are restricted from their full potential
They're concerned about food, water, shelter, or other things they see as more essential
When you're stuck in just your point of view, your life alone
Just remember there are still pains out there you are fortunate to have never known.

13.

Some say words don't suffice, they aren't enough
But sometimes what you say to me becomes too much
I think and overthink everything you've ever said
Because the thought of you leaving me is something
I'll always dread
See, it's never been easy for me to trust since people
tend to come and go
I believe them, they leave, and I have nothing to show
Of the love they pretended to have for me
Of the words they said to set me free.

14.

Let's go back, go back to the streets of Brooklyn
When the times were simpler and the days were longer
Where your dreams were newer and your faith was stronger
You started your life from nothing, yet none of that held much bearing
Because you were never judged for how you spoke or what you were wearing
You focused on your goals and what you wanted to achieve
All you needed to do was work hard and believe
Only to leave the people you called your own
Only to abandon the neighborhoods you had once known
So let's go back to where you were before
Go up the old stoop steps, the foundation from where you soared.

15.

Sometimes I don't realize how much you've changed me
Sometimes I don't realize without you how empty I would be
Because it's crazy to think, I never thought it would be true
You mean so much to me that I find myself praying for you.

16.

Self-talk: when an individual converses with herself to find peace
Because she doesn't feel whole, she's missing a piece
The world around her is overwhelming and unfair
There are lives being lost, wars being fought, and no time for a prayer
Her home country is in pain, crying loudly
It feels a lot different from when she used to stand up in her classroom, and recite its pledge proudly
Land of the free, home of the brave
Now seems to be a land suffering, every day digging a new grave.

17.

Never be afraid of yourself
Your skin color, your hometown, your religion
These things may define parts of your life but they don't define how you should be treated
They shouldn't be determinants of how bright your future is going to be or if you can reach your full potential
Because we were given our lives for a reason
Each living, breathing entity has a purpose and is worth more than you can imagine
You're worth more than you can imagine
Never be afraid, fear is just a tactic being used
That makes these violent acts go unnoticed and easily excused.

18.

I did it all for you
My past is dedicated to you
Because the things I did, the life I lead was for your satisfaction
Everything you hated was banned, called a distraction
I didn't question because you said you had your reasons
Following you was as common as the change of the seasons
I even climbed the highest mountains, braved the roaring thunder
Faced my deepest fears for you but did you ever wonder?
That I was never really living, merely alive
Cut off from the world around me, passion deprived.

19.

Respect isn't something that just comes out of nowhere
Then why do you think you can just apologize from thin air?
I don't remember words ever meaning more than your action
But I do remember being treated like a monetary transaction
Because I never meant anything more to you than a check off the list
And now you're coming back and saying it's me you missed
Well, your time is up, oh, it was long gone
Now that perfect picture of us that you had drawn
Is meaningless to me just like your stupid excuses
I sincerely hope my words left some bumps and some bruises.

20.

Patience
For our instant pleasure generation this seems to be a dying trait
Giving people a chance seems much harder than giving them hate
Our own points of view matter more because they hit close to home
If others want to reap the benefits they should conform
Because what's different is unnecessary
The burden of individuality is too heavy to carry
Patience is considered weakness because the physical fighter is revered the most
It's a virtue that takes time and can't be acquired through a single social media post
Judgment is consuming our minds and fogging our vision
Instigating violence and encouraging division.

21.

Being thankful is easy when everything is going well
When heaven seems a lot more real than hell
But when life changes and the clouds turn dark
It only takes a second to lose that spark
Because being grateful for what we have seems more attainable when we have it all
It's hard to remember that the higher the goal the steeper the fall
What has been taken from you wasn't part of your story
Wasn't part of your path to glory
So be thankful for the here and now
The good, the bad, the ugly makes us stronger even if we don't know how.

22.

Before you criticize her past remember how you live today
Before you criticize her words remember your free speech
Before you strip her of her honor remember who gave you those powerful hands
Before you push her off her pedestal remember who lifted you up
It is so easy to say she didn't do what was right, she didn't have a progressive plan
But did you ever stop to think if you would have expected the same if she was a man?
Too often our society expects a woman of her time to risk it all for the sake of womanhood
We forget that in her times she was probably doing all that she could
For her family, her country, and rarely herself.

23.

It was never meant to be this way
It shouldn't be that hard to make you stay
With me in times of weakness, in times of pain
You taught me to brave the storm and dance in the rain
Because life is too short for me to worry about every little thing
Only if you provoke it will the bee sting
You told me my trusting nature was a curse and a blessing
There are a lot of people that want to stop me from progressing
These cautionary words that used to frustrate me
Are now distant reminders of your memory
Of the effect you've had on my daily routine
That have left me to only have faith in the unseen.

24.

Unapologetically I rise from the ashes
As the fire distinguishes and the thunder crashes
God knows I've been through this before
You know you've thrown me on the floor
When I rose higher than you could take
When you were finally exposed as a fake
Emerging from the smoke that once fogged my vision
Taking advantage of the force from that head-first collision
Determination in one hand and pride in another
Raging on with the strength of no other.

25.

People say it's easier to love a perfect God
To fall for the unblemished being that can do no wrong
This is why unconditional love towards a human is far more frightening and difficult
Humans make mistakes and have countless imperfections
Fixing them requires patience and devotion
However, you'll know it's real love when all the imperfections seem too perfect to correct
It's just a matter of whether those flaws are worth the risk to protect.

26.

I know that sometimes you forget to help yourself
Because helping others just seems too important, more
of a priority
But you don't have to sacrifice your happiness for
someone else
Yes, helping others is a necessity but so is your own
sanity
Living your life, loving yourself will bring you one step
closer to uplifting those around you
If you can be thankful for every thorn in your life,
you'll be more inclined to see the rose
You won't have to go out of your way to help others,
it'll just naturally show.

27.

They say change is constant
That you should be ready for life's twists and turns
Fight through the growing pains even if it burns
Because life is full surprises and not everything is forever
But what if I want it to last?
I want something to stay even though I never asked
For it to consume me a great deal
For it to change the way I feel
But I guess this change is ok with me
Because it makes me feel alive, it sets me free.

28.

When one door closes another appears
Sometimes the slam seems so abrupt that it can't help but ignite your fears
Because what is on the horizon is new and daunting
You can just hear the sounds of failure, all their taunting
But what you don't know yet is what has been done is for your own good
You shouldn't stop the door from closing even if you could
Life isn't about the small endings and the short-lived experiences
It's about your overall journey and what you learned
Not about how quickly you sank but how incredibly you returned.

29.

Did you ever do anything other than complain?
Yes, maybe during the sunshine but how about the rain?
When the thunder was crashing and too heavy bear
Did you ever do something more than criticize and scare?
Because right now we don't need someone to give us a negative state of affairs
But someone who listens, finds solutions, someone who actually cares
I know that respecting and empathizing with others seems like a given
That a leader should roll with the punches and be driven
But unfortunately nowadays power isn't given to leaders but merely to those with leadership positions
That yell, insult, and make rash, selfish decisions
So let me not only hear your calls for a movement
But let me also see your actions in pursuit for a better world, for an improvement.

30.

Educated people making reckless decisions
Not bringing the community together but creating divisions
Were those years in the classroom worth it?
Did you not learn to persevere and not quit?
Not quit on those who might need a little more support
Who crave justice but the last place they'll get it is in court
Because this system is created only to help those who can afford the pain
All the money in the world can't take back the emotional drain
Did you ever think about that when you saw an innocent man lay everything on the line?
Or did they not teach you that in the textbook pages you were assigned?
In that classroom where you vowed to make a change
Little did you know for a hefty paycheck, morality you would exchange.

31.

The world can be a cruel place
I won't always be first in this race
But there is always one person that loves me no matter what
She is someone that protected me from harsh realities when I was young
Who tells me to clean my room and watch my tongue
Because she wants me to be the best version of me
I was once a part of her but there comes a time where she must set me free
She has raised me as the confident and strong woman her own mother was
So in this fast paced life I must remember to stop and pause
For she is the one who knows me the best
To see her, to love her, to hold her I am truly blessed
She is my mother, my Amma.

32.

The ground is shaking, hearts are breaking, people are feeling hopeless, and then I see you
Your eyes deceive me into thinking I can get through
The pains of the world don't seem to bother me in your arms
All the things that should knock me down, shake my core, don't even raise an alarm
Because I know even through all the bitterness and the hate, one thing rings true
When the smoke clears and my eyes widen I'll see you
Looking at me with that smile I can't get out of my mind
Holding the very glimmer of hope I've been trying to find.

33.

Sometimes you'll feel like you're in a cell
The world's closing in too quickly and no one around you can really tell
Because you keep it inside so it won't burden people around you
They can't possibly understand what you're going through
The thoughts, the scenarios that they think of
Are your reality, they are beyond their imagination
It doesn't just come and go but it stays leaving a permanent sensation
When you're around that person, that thing, that place
You remember the emotional rollercoaster you faced
But now it's time to become a new
It's not about what's been done but about what you will do.

34.

I thought out of everyone you would understand
I thought you would remember after everything we
had planned
You would keep your word and stay with me
It feels more like betrayal than setting me free
But there's no point in crying over what is done
Because in this battle of happiness you have won
Now I must pick myself up piece by piece
Remember this not as abandonment but as sweet
release.

35.

I think about you almost every single day
I write these words to help the pain go away
Because loving you was incredible in every single way
It broke my heart and lead me astray
God gave me you so I wasn't afraid
For those small moments of joy, it was a big price to pay
But to remember those times forever I will always pray
Because even if I willingly left I will always want you, I will always want to stay.

36.

What was I supposed to do?
When your waves crashed a little too hard and drenched me in your lies
When your comforting breeze broke down my walls, a relentless wind in disguise
If I'm being honest I wasn't expecting this great of a storm
If I'm being candid it was quite a show for you to perform
Pretending that you were a God-sent blessing
Not an unpredictable force that would leave me guessing
Wondering if I was the one to blame
Finding myself hopelessly lost in the eye of the hurricane.

37.

It was kind of scary
Not because you were left alone but because he was with you
Because you could be with him
You didn't have to call for him to have him running to you
You didn't have to beg for him to smile at you
It was kind of scary
Not because you wanted to leave but because you wanted to stay
Not because you were forgetting him but because for him you would always pray
It was kind of scary
Not because he left you but because you were lacing up your running shoes
To leave the person who was giving you too much ease
It was hard for you to believe that this was real and not a tease
I guess it stopped being so scary
Because you let go of your past
Because you laced up your shoes but to him you ran so fast.

38.

I know you're afraid
I know you don't know where to turn
Because you thought you knew but you had much to learn
About the people around you and the world we live in
Hesitated to pray to God because of how long it's been
Didn't know if he would even listen because these days it seems like no one will
People preach acceptance but will it really work if it's against your will?
Against everything you stand for, the fiber of your being
Anger and prejudice is all you're seeing
I want you to know that goodness is still calling out
As hard as it is don't focus on those who refuse speak the language of love
Because when they go low, we rise above.

39.

I am somebody
Somebody that walks these streets same as you
Somebody with a love for this country so true
So why do you antagonize me and assign blame
For these horrid actions and accusations, I didn't ask for this kind of fame
For the longest time I never went out of my way, didn't think I had anything to say
Because I was hushed too many times to want to stay
Now in a time where explicit discrimination is made okay
Where the highest offices don't represent me
Do you expect me to feel as free?
As your sacred constitution teaches
As your holy God preaches
I am not just a color I am not just a number
I am allowed to speak my mind just like any other
Express my ideas, the ones like no other.

40.

"Brother pray for our Muslim people"
"Sister pray for our Christian people"
"They need us, OUR people need us"
The sincerest of sentiments seem like the most segregated of them all
Only thinking of one group, recognizing one downfall
We forget that human souls are merely taught religious division, not born with it
We forget we are all made of the same blood and flesh
Why do we choose only to pray for the people of our faith?
The almighty has created all, he loves all he saith
So put your judgment away because people are dying
Don't use a Facebook post as a form of trying
Don't go into the world hoping to convert
Try to heal around you with your actions because right now the world is hurt
Started by a problem heavily grown
The question of who gave us life, the greatest unknown.

41.

Making a living selling dope
Because taking it sometimes feels like hope
That you won't be in this trash of a home
That you won't feel this damn alone
In the dark where fears creep in
Where the scars left were deeper than skin
Where there was no faith and you were destined for doom
So keep smoking that substance till it fills the room
Because love never came that easy
To you or the ones in your neighborhood
You didn't know all the things that you should
Your grades, the books you read didn't judge how tall you stood
It was all about the cool kids and crowded hallways
where you felt like your life was on the line
So take that pill as a sign to close your eyes and hope it'll all be fine.

42.

Don't tell me you're scared of what people might say, what people might think
Don't crawl into isolation, don't let your strong opinions shrink
Because life was made for you to not only live and let live
But for you to find peace and happiness in the love and compassion you give
The happiest people don't always have the most money
The smartest don't always have the highest degrees
But the ones at ease are those who refuse to let their fear stop them from making this world a better place
You wouldn't have been put on this earth if there wasn't enough space
For your beauty, for your creativity, the almighty makes no mistakes
So fight for your dreams, reach for the impossible no matter how high the stakes.

43.

When politics turns into comedy the biggest clown wins
So bring on the jokes to mask your sins
The government is a show and our lives are the main act
Playing games with us, expecting us to react
In the most negative way to prove you were right all along
That we are a bunch of idiots, everything we do is wrong
We don't deserve your freedoms, your rights
Well before you touch this girl just know she bites
She bites back at those who jest her very existence
As she hears the jokers laughing in the distance.

44.

Of course God is good
But is that an excuse to not stand up for all the things
that you should?
Everyone around me just leaving it up to the almighty
taking no action of their own
You really think God is going to call your phone?
To tell you to be a good person and make a change
Oh no, talking to him is a whole other kind of
exchange
It is not what is heard, it is not what is said
It is what you felt and what life you led
So don't tell me whatever will be will be
Go pray because guidance comes from faith in what
we can't see.

45.

No, I'm not fighting for a right that was recently taken away
I'm fighting for the social norms that make it okay
Okay to rate a woman on a scale, both the beauty and the weight kind
I'm fighting for girls who feel they will never be taken seriously no matter how hard they grind
They don't realize that we don't wear makeup for them, we don't dress up for them
We don't get degrees just to find and marry a rich one of them
We go for ourselves and the betterment of our lives
To show we can earn more than the title of wives
You can take your inequality and leave it in past
After all, God created Eve after Adam, saving the best for last.

46.

Never be too hard on yourself when something doesn't go right
When it feels like what you initially wanted isn't worth the fight
Because life isn't a sprint, quick and then it's done
It's a marathon, you might have to change your pace but keep a steady run
So don't overthink the anxiety in your life and all the stress
After all, if we didn't have hardships, how could we ever differentiate failure from success.

47.

Please don't ask about my heart
It doesn't belong to its owner
Shouldn't have told him I was an organ donor
Yeah I'm sure he'll give it back to me someday
Just as soon as I throw his perfect image away
So where did that love go, as bright as the stars?
Oh it was never really here, never really ours.

48.

My fire didn't stop when you extinguished the flame
Now my spirit can't be tamed
Because I was put here for a purpose, a reason
Like a tree, my leaves can change with the season
But my roots keep me grounded, make me strong
They will help me change the world and prove you wrong.

49.

Once in a blue moon I think of you
Once in a blue moon I forget we're through
Once in a while I ask myself why
Once in a while I remember that high
The one that lifted me off my feet
The one that felt so bittersweet
Once in a while I remember I won't see you soon
But darling, that's only once in a while,
That's only once in a blue moon.

50.

Why do you see yourself as so small?
Why do you bend for those who step on others to feel tall?
I want you to know you have a purpose, that this is your life
I want you to know that your intellect is sharper than any knife
You were chosen to walk this Earth and be the very best you
Not to be a robot and respond to every command, every cue
Your mind is beautiful; it's a place filled with love
You deserve to be all that you've dreamed of
You don't have to prove anything to anyone
You can dance, sing, and chase the sun
Because life is worth living, especially for someone as extraordinary as you
So stop for a moment, take a deep breath, and enjoy the view.

51.

I didn't think I was up for it
Didn't think I was good enough
God gave me this life and it's meant to be tough
I have to reach for the goals of those that have come before
The ones that leave me empty, begging for more
They leave me wandering the world in search of a bigger truth
An impossible venture, my fountain of youth
Something that would emerge from the darkness, show its beauty in the light
Maybe someone who would tell me I was finally doing something right.

52.

Our lives are not defined by the actions done with ease
We are defined by the days, the moments, and the words we seize
A time filled with pain and inevitable sorrow
Is a just a precaution warning us to make a better tomorrow
United we must stand with strength and grace
To show we are all meant for greatness and not just occupying space.

53.

He changed me
And just like a rose I became
Red as fire, sharp as a blade
Waiting for this fantasy to go up in flames
Waiting for you to realize you could have more
I'm not the best you could have, of that I'm sure
I'm waiting for that look you give with your head tilted
To be a distant memory of a rose now wilted.

54.

God gave me you and I didn't know why
It's not like this could end in anything but goodbye
I'm always one to plan what is ahead and constantly pray
Never would I have thought I would want something so temporary to stay
But now that short lived spark has dwindled to smoke
Filling the space in this heart you just broke.

55.

These torn lives, these chaotic storms
Have become our reality, our idea of social norms
So remember your etiquette when the armed come charging in
Calm the fast beating hearts of those who haven't sinned
Because in this world there's no morality, it isn't clear
Whether the person in front of you will leave you with hope or shake you with fear
Their brisk pace shouldn't be alarming
They look at you with the same grin you once found charming
With a house, a car, a home cooked meal you were pleased
Now cater to them until their bigoted wishes are appeased.

56.

And just like a flower I was gleaming in the sunlight
In a cluster of my own, till I was torn, out of sight
Whether this change would be fruitful only time would tell
At first I was taken care of, not a petal out of place
Not after long, my stems withered, lost their green
My leaves had lost their luminous sheen
Until my whole figure was browned, and down-turned
Until it was too late for a lesson well-learned.

57.

Insecurities that bring on hate
Risking the lives of the same millions, oh their twisted fate
Told not to be offended, not to be scared
Showing their false sympathy, as if they ever cared
About the lives lost, about the years of hatred
Embracing our flag that they hold so sacred
Forgetting its meaning, treating others as scum
Forgetting the foreign countries their ancestors came from
No this isn't about jobs, this isn't about immigration
This is about keeping their superiority in our belovéd nation
As they walk with torches in their hands, full of conviction
It's time to face the reality we once saw as fiction.

58.

You don't know what I'd do to hang on to your love
Over all worldly things I hold it above
It keeps me sane, it keeps me true
I see the blue skies in a whole different hue
You don't know what I'd do, what I would give
Because dying for you I learned how to live.

59.

The more I try to face you, the more I feel afraid
The words you spew, the hate you bring are hitting harder than any blade
These tears that run down my face are not a sign of weakness
They are a product of all the nights that have gone by distraught and speechless
Thinking about whether my future can be depended on, whether I'm ready to move past
Have you done all the damage or are you saving the worst for last?
Because these days I'm not surprised, I'm not fazed by the truth
As you walk to your throne stepping on all those like me
You'll realize there are too many of us, from sea to shining sea.

60.

I'm just looking for something to hold on to
I'm just looking for something more
I'm just looking for my forever
I'm just looking for something to shake my core
I'm just hoping for someone who becomes my moon
I'm just hoping for someone to become my stars
I'm just hoping for someone who fills this void soon
I'm just hoping to change my mine to ours
I'm just worried that no one will know me well enough
I'm just worried God might not hear my dreams
I'm just worried that I won't find my strength when times are tough
I'm just worried no one will be bothered when I'm breaking at the seams
I'm just calm because no one can see the storm
I'm just calm because of the love around me
I'm just calm because one day the ice will become warm
I'm just calm because no strings are attached, I'm unapologetically free.

61.

When I saw you, my heart shattered
Spread all across that room, in disarray it was scattered
I hadn't seen you in a while, thought this pain had passed
I didn't want this feeling, it's not what I asked
I'm tied up here, you're tied up there
It wouldn't be life if it played fair
It just didn't work out the way we wanted it to
But knowing you was never regretful, because I experienced a love so true
A love so deep the universe would drown in its own envy
Even in that time you were next to me
Holding my hand, telling me I'm worth more
Those memories, with my heart, are still scattered across the floor.

62.

I didn't want you now because it hurt too much
I didn't want you now because my heart's cold to the touch
From all I'd been through, I didn't expect you to understand
What comes over me when you look my way or hold my hand
I was filled with the anxiety of experience and hopefulness of what was to come
When you get too close how am I supposed to calm my heart that beats like a drum
It's a paradox, a perfect storm, one I might have surrendered to
And into the ghastly winds I flew, all the way back to you.

63.

Turning every corner looking for your face
I crave that security, I remember your embrace
So tight, so right, you never let go
It felt like I was tucked in the largest blanket
It was like I was given the elixir of faith and I drank it
Every last drop until I thought
This country was progressing, I was blind to the wrought
But ignorance waits for no one and it was time to move, the show must go on
So here I am ready to bring you back, tears in my eyes, sword drawn.

64.

You expected one thing from me, I expected another
Your well-intentioned hug felt more like a smother
That stopped me from breathing, but I didn't have the courage to let go
I was always taught that I needed to sacrifice and just go with the flow
Now it's getting too hard for me, my love, hard for me to stay
Neither of us knew it would turn out this way
We were blinded by lust and motivated by security
Our fiery love has now become an unforgettable obscurity.

65.

Your eyes captured me in such a daze
I was lost in them and fell victim to their maze
People ask me why, they don't understand the truth
They have no idea what it's like to be in love with you.

66.

I feel like my life is going miles at a time
Everyday another battle to fight, another mountain to climb
And then there's you
With you it feels effortless, I could talk for hours
I feel as if you're ready to take on my struggles as yours, as ours
And so I'm standing, here, in this crowded street waiting for that feeling
Ready to gain back the sanity you're stealing
With every look, every smile
I'm ready to stop time, and with you, walk each mile.

67.

I met you and I felt this urge
I felt this wind, I felt this surge
Of emotions I didn't know I still had
Of thoughts that made me mad
For thinking I was worth less than I am
That love wasn't real and it was all a sham
But these lies will dictate me no longer
Because with every breath you take, I become stronger.

68.

See that fluorescent light flicker
Feel the tension in the air becoming thicker
Waiting patiently for the decision to change your life
Whether you'd have to take the bullet or fall on the knife
Because in your world there isn't much of a happy ending
No grand prize for all this time your spending
So you wait in this room as the light starts to spark
Before you know it, your world stops, and the light goes dark.

69.

Expect the worst, hope for the best
Imagine the craziest, do something no one would've guessed
Be different, be real, be someone you'd love
Be down to earth, but pray above
Learn to forgive, try to forget
There's a reason for everyone you've met
Don't let anyone stop you from expressing your truth
Live fully at every age, don't search for physical youth
You were given just one life as you are
Experience everything and learn from each and every scar.

70.

God gave me you so I guess it's ok
That I can't really get my sanity to stay
Who needs reality when you're my dream
Who needs commitment when we're breaking at the seam
So hold me until my heart is broken
Talk to me until every last word is spoken
And I'll just listen as my eyes slowly close
Accepting this ending because that's how life goes.

71.

They say we're made in pairs
But where is my other half to peel back the layers
To know every inch of me
And set my insecurity free
Honestly, I've been waiting longer than I can
Just finding solace in it being God's plan.

72.

Put my voice on the speaker to make sure everyone hears
Do you think somehow I can conceal my tears?
Checking the mic, one, two, one, two
I hope you know this one's for you
Because you gave me that light where darkness didn't exist
But somehow I loved you and lost myself in the midst
All I knew is you were my sun and around you I traveled
I didn't realize that the orbit left a trail of me unraveled
So here I am in this mic speaking my mind
Telling you the problems I decided to leave behind.

73.

I know it feels like the world is falling apart
I know you want to forget the past but you just don't
have the heart
There's just too much to remember, too much to feel
Those memories open your wounds every time they
try to heal
But life is filled with shocks, filled with change
Sometimes you'll get happiness and sometimes you'll
get pain
So leave behind the impossible possibilities and focus
on what you've known
That it's not about how or why it all fell apart but
about how much you've grown.

74.

Point a gun to my heart and pull the trigger quick
I rather be gone and silenced than living and sick
Sick of the way you spit on my name
Sick of the way you mask your bias and say mental illness is to blame
I kick myself for being surprised
That you would ignore the pain and support the research you once chastised
So bring on the fake support for the well-being of the people you could care less about
As you lay in your ocean of hypocrisy in this never ending drought.

75.

I know you want to live your life, chase those crazy thrills
But you know that taking a risk won't pay the bills
Because what is a life of choice when there's nowhere to hide
From this vicious cycle, no matter how much you cried, no matter how many people died
All that's left is hope in your heart and faith in your creator
Looking to the sky, hoping for something greater
Just know you can speak your mind and you will conquer this pain
You might have some to lose but you have so much more to gain.

76.

It's kind of hard for me to believe
That you're doing what's best for me when I just want to leave
Your stubbornness has kept me in a choke hold
I need to respect you and your decisions, like I've been told
But when does the time come for you to see
That my life is my life and no one else's to live
That you take more from me than you give
So here I am with an open heart and a strong stance
Waiting for you to listen and give me just one chance
To speak my mind and let you know
That I am capable of far more than I show.

77.

It has me feeling some type of way
It has me wondering why I even stay
Where the bullets are free and the children are enslaved
Where being ignorant is synonymous to being well behaved
So let the gun smoke fill the hearts of the ones who've lost
Easy access to a trigger is worth the cost
It has me feeling some type of way
That a place meant for knowledge and play
Has become an institution of pain and fear
They believe a machine is worth all the tears
Because who needs an education when no students are left
Their 2nd Amendment freedom has committed the ultimate theft
It has me feeling some type of way
When they protect deadly weapons and then to the Lord they pray
To the same Lord who preaches love and compassion

But, of course, they choose to separate him from their actions
They say they're conservative but what are they conserving?
Just the constant pain of the ones undeserving
It has me feeling some type of way
And that's all I really have to say.

78.

Thankful for the family I have
The life I live
Thankful for the free speech I have
The songs I sing
Thankful for the trees, the moon, the stars
And all that you are
Thankful I got to see you live your best life
Succeed with no hesitation
Thankful I didn't stop myself
I gave into temptation
Thankful that not all tempting things are dangerous
And that God made a plan for you, for me, for us.

79.

I really took for granted all that you are
I really didn't realize the distance was this far
Until it was time to pack my bags and leave your embrace
Until it was time to go where every day I couldn't see your face
I know this is good for me and this is what you raised me to do
You tell me to believe in myself and follow my dreams too
But what will I do after a long, stressful week if I can't put my hand in your palm?
What will I do when the world becomes too much and I just need my mom?
I've gotta stay strong for you and for me
Because I'm trying to be everything you are and everything you want me to be
So I'll try not to be sad thinking I'm doing this for you
As I walk around the big city making big decisions while I think, "What would Amma do?"

80.

He told her she couldn't
He told her she shouldn't
He told her it won't work
He told her this with a smirk
He told her he knows what's best
He told her he'll handle the rest
He told her it worked through dumb luck
He told her it's only time she gets stuck
He told her this success was "for the both of us"
He told her in her ideas he would always trust
He told her not to leave, she wouldn't find better
He told her he would finally write her that love letter
He told her he would change like the coins she turned to stacks
She told him to leave and turned her back
Head held high
Wings spread to fly.

81.

Sometimes the city lights shine a little brighter
Sometimes the wind embraces my face a little tighter
Sometimes I feel a comforting energy as if God is sitting next to me
Sometimes I don't know whether I should jump with joy or get down on my knees
I felt this change when I met you
You took this old street and made it brand new
Your beauty spread through the depths of these buildings, in each and every part
You showed me my life wasn't over, you were just the start
The beginning of a journey to feed the soul
An endless climb to not only find my other half, but to become, within myself, whole.

82.

Two ships crossing at night
Refusing to acknowledge the tension within sight
We both feel the waves crash and the slight sway of the sea
It's hard to believe that we were once one vessel, it was once just you and me
It was a time where we experienced the world together
It was a time where I saw the stars twinkle in your eyes, regardless of the weather
Now we're just two ships crossing at night
Blinded by our independence, blinded by the lack of light.

83.

The heart longs for what the mind can't comprehend
You keep opening those wounds, you won't let them mend
With every look, with every smile you light me up
Who needs this coffee when you fill my cup?
What can I say? I was a hopeless cynic
You've made me what I wasn't, a hopeful romantic.

84.

I remember the day I felt safe
I remember the day like it was yesterday
The sky was blue, the path was clear
I held my mother's hand out of desire not fear
God knows I can't go back to how it once was
And I know I need to live in the present because
The past has trapped me for the last time
Being me is not a sin, it's not a crime
Because I look different, because I'm not the same
My words will put them all to shame.

85.

I sit in this café seeing the world in fast forward
People coming and going, trying to find some certainty in this uncertain life
Whether it be a specific coffee order or social media persona
They want to let people know they are certain, consistent, and most importantly, that they exist
As I watch the cars pass by, the horns in the distance
Signaling this sense of urgency that they assume will die with the press of a button
As I watch the light of the sky slowly transition through the small cracks of the tall buildings
I think that this natural course does not alert anyone of its beauty
Nor does it feel the need to tell everyone it is special
It just is
This beauty needs no notification, no affirmation to remain consistent, to remain free
It thrives in its uncertainty and no one expects anything more
So why do we?

86.

Meeting you was like listening to my favorite song for the first time
Lasting only a couple minutes until I knew you were mine
I listened to you over and over but it would never get old
Your notes in repetition spoke to me, with every lyric told
Until one day I hit play and my mistake and drifted
You faded into the background and my feelings shifted
I used to relish every rhythm, every beat
Now I have no desire to click repeat
So I might hear you in my car on a long trip
And finally have the courage to press skip.

87.

Take it all in, the different shades
Breathe in patience, and breathe out their blades
Filled with hate, filled with doubt
That we won't be listened to unless we scream and shout
Told we are to be seen not heard
The line between ignorance and orthodoxy has been blurred
You might hand them a mirror to give them some direction
But don't be surprised if they destroy it, not being able to face their own reflection
It shows them the world's not just black and white
It's filled with every color, every hue shining so bright
Our differences are making life traumatic
Rather than embracing reality as being prismatic.

88.

I don't want to miss those days
The darkness left but the feeling stays
I'm motionless with emotions running through my brain
Wishing I didn't catch that train
Because then I wouldn't be reminded of what could be
Now I'm trying to find the sanity you stole from me
God blessed me with a beautiful, painful paradox
Even when my mouth is closed this heart still talks
It sings your song, it memorized your blues
Knowing very well either way it would lose.

89.

She didn't know this wasn't her place
She didn't know it would only take a taste
To fall so quickly into his eyes
She found the truth through all his lies
When the damage had been done, the words had been spoken
She still felt the most comfort in something so broken
He brought her the intensity she lacks
This ever consuming feeling was worth a few cracks
So she kept the pain, to which she would forever be tied
Because he always loved how beautiful she looked when she cried.

90.

She fell because he made her feel wanted
She was never something he advertised, never something he flaunted
She gave up her sanity, while he was unfazed
She was holding on to something unreal, caught in a daze
She told herself she wouldn't fall because she grasped on to reality so tight
Little did she know she would descend so quick, never catching flight
Now she's left confused as to why it took so long
Sifting through all his rights to find what went wrong.

91.

The show comes to a close with the drawing of the velvet curtain
Leaving behind an open-ended fate, a future uncertain
The script was followed, the lines were spoken
Yet you can't help but feel so broken
Because you worked this hard and it wasn't enough
To appease the crowd so cruel, so tough
You doubt your talent, you doubt your skills
Your heart beats fast and with pain it fills
Knowing you might never be fit for the role
For the sake of the performance you sold your soul.

92.

Did things really have to change?
When I told you I loved you, was it really that strange?
To think that I could look at you and the whole world would fade
To think that every night I fell to my knees and prayed
That this feeling would disintegrate because I wasn't meant to feel this way
But in all this black and white, you were my gray
The part of my life so uncertain, so unknown
Being without you, I felt so alone
Because I defined myself as a product of your attention
But did all of that have to change with the feelings I mentioned?
I would say I take it back but that would be a lie
Who knew this would end in your goodbye?

93.

Always said I didn't need your touch
Didn't know I would miss your smile so much
Kept this hard exterior because that's who I thought I was
Till you broke me down, till I turned to dust
Brushed off my pain with a grin
The purest of passions felt like a sin
The fear of intimacy made me suffer alone
Until this fiery passion turned cold as stone.

94.

Big girls don't cry
Big girls also think it's easier to lie
About their feelings because it's no one else's issue
That they're up all night drowning their sorrows in a tissue
Men might use those tears as ammunition
Not as a part of human nature but as a definition
Confining women by their emotions is nothing new
This is the same old darkness but just a different hue.

95.

If you'd ask for the stars, I would've given you the moon
Brought a constellation to my world of dust and had me swoon
Told me my universe would be lit up by the bright light of your star
Made me crave your elements, all that you are
My orbit depended on your energy, I was deeply bound
Until you broke that connection, without making a sound
The stratosphere surrounding me shattered and hollow was my soul
Never being able to forget as I fall into this black hole.

96.

You were always told to work for the next big thing
Whether it be a degree, a job, maybe a man and a diamond ring
They don't want you to relish the present because the future easily insights fear
They threaten you that you will lose everything you hold dear
Your passion project turned into a schedule so mundane
It's easier to work in monotony than take a risk that might cause pain
So break this cycle of predictability and do something wild
With the strength of a woman but the curiosity of a child.

97.

Growing up you noticed your differences more than what made you the same
You were embarrassed by the complexities of your culture, any time someone would mispronounce your name
You thought life would be easier if you didn't look this way
If your hair was a little straighter and your body was a little thinner maybe this feeling of emptiness would go away
This feeling was fragile, kept your heart on your sleeve
Your father always said you were beautiful but it was getting too hard to believe
That something so different could ever be admired
Telling everyone you were fine had you a little tired
Calling you brave for loving yourself turned you numb
As if your appearance was an obstacle you so courageously had to overcome
I'm here to tell you it's normal to be unique
Everyone feels different but that doesn't make you weak.

Your differences are your power and will take you far
Stop waiting for others to notice and fully fall in love
with yourself for all that you are.

98.

You are a forced to be reckoned with, a never ending fire
Then why do you let mere sparks diminish your desire
Your craving for something more, your lust for success
Ignore their doubts, never settle for less
You don't need "the perfection" they try to sell
Walk away from the negativity, wishing them well.

99.

You left your past to be mine
You left me shackled in what was while you enjoy
telling everyone you're fine
I don't want to believe it to be true because our
memories replay in my mind like a movie
I ignore reality and am consumed not by who we are
but who we were supposed to be.

100.

Here you are living every day, bringing peace to other people's lives
You were told your purpose was marriage, after all, speckled skin girls make good wives
Yes you can have a career but only to make you more desirable in the eyes of a man
No one ever let you think this was a matter of if you want, not if you can
Your body is treated like a boxing bag until it's time to reproduce
Then once you produced the fruit of your labor it's said to have lost its use
I cry for you and how you overlook your beauty and worth
I wish you knew you were created to offer so much more to this Earth.

101.

You said you like them blonde
Well I could go on and on
About how we're better together
The way my heart beats when you lean in is something out of a dream
You know coffee is always better with a little cream
Don't tell me you don't feel it too
I'll go numb because all I feel is you.

102.

Tired of trying to please everyone
Tired of stunting my growth for those who refuse to watch me succeed
Tired of giving people the benefit of the doubt when they don't do the same for me
Tired masking who I truly am just to make others comfortable
Tired of people invalidating emotions as if that fosters growth
Tired of being labeled as something before I even open my mouth
Tired of living life as an optimist
Tired of trying
Yet I'll keep trying for the ones who come after me.

103.

No, I wasn't pretending to be someone else, I wasn't putting on a show
I wasn't trying to be noticed, but I just want to know
How you found the beauty in me in this crowded room
How could someone like you with a smile like that making all the girls swoon
Lock eyes with a girl like me being unapologetically me
How could one glance set all my worries free?

104.

Didn't realize how much we drifted apart
Maybe we both felt this distance but we didn't leave,
we didn't have the heart
It took our friends canceling on us and sitting alone in
this 5th floor walk up to hear the silence so loud
It was so easy to over schedule ourselves so our
problems could get lost in the crowd
Maybe we should end this now before we face our
inevitable doom
Or maybe we just lay here, two lost souls in this silent
room.

105.

You've felt this emptiness all your life
You look to the cosmos to blame for your strife
Because the one who was going to take away all your pain should have made an appearance by now
You keep looking in the eyes of couples thinking "how?"
How did they find love so fast?
In this never ending race for true bliss how did I end up last?
You find yourself caught in a daze, creating fantasies just so you have something to feel
Then reality sets in and you mourn the loss of someone who isn't even real.

106.

Would you have loved me if I gave in to your
unforgiving smolder?
Would you have loved me if I listened to the devil on
my shoulder?
Telling me to gamble it all for the sake of our spark
Forever flickering never knowing whether I'll be lit up
or left in the dark
I've been down this road before and I think I've had
my fix
My heart will no longer be nailed on to your crucifix.

107.

I talked into the sky today hoping to get some answers
The stars and planets winked at me and moved like tiny dancers
I sat there alone trying to understand what this all meant and why I'm even here
Until the clouds were set in motion uncovering the moon lending her ear
I indulged her in my theories of life trying not to shake in her mighty sight
I don't think I ever got a response from her or maybe it was the distance and the height
But I felt this greater sense of purpose, more than what the material world would permit
Left me thinking that maybe there's light at the end, maybe this is all worth it.

108.

Learning to love myself before I loved you never seemed like a option me
I thought giving my all to you was the only way you wouldn't leave
Little did I know we'd soon realize how far apart we'd grown
And You would leave, taking all my self worth with you, leaving me all alone.

109.

I watched as you betrayed me in the name of lust
I thought no one else would understand Nomads like us
So we would be bound together as the fates desire
Little did I know you would turn out to be such a liar
You never once regretted leaving me for her
Left me wandering this desert alone in search of something greater
How do I still let it consume me if I knew it wouldn't last?
How do I continue to view our love through cherry colored glass?

110.

You broke down this hard exterior leaving me exposed
I thought I was meant to be strong because that's just
how life goes
But not when I'm around you
Not when I'm around your contagious spirit that could
light up the darkest night
Not when I can release this anxiety that has boiled up
inside me, all this pent up fright
You are the sweetest release, the only thing keeping
me sane
I just hope this bliss doesn't end in lasting pain.

III.

She never felt beautiful, she never felt like she
belonged
She didn't know how it felt to have someone admire
her beauty
She only knew how it felt to have someone admire her
strength for existing in her natural form
She was never considered conventional or normal
She never knew how it felt to be a threat to anyone
else
She never felt sexy or confident, she felt like a token
An object used to show differences can be acceptable
She always felt like she was replaceable
Like a woman of western decent mimicking her
features could take her place any minute
Because no one actually ever wanted her in her purest
form
They just want someone who looks similar but didn't
come with the cultural baggage.

112.

I didn't want to leave, but you forced my hand
I didn't want to drop to my knees, but you made it hard to stand
You told me it was too much to take as if my steadfast support was a weight you couldn't bear anymore
But who do you think this soul crushing, never wavering support was for?
You acted as if you were doing me a favor sticking around
Even though I asked you if I was too much and you said I was sunshine you just one day found
In that moment I knew what people meant by actions over words
Because you sang such a beautiful song, till you flew away with the snowbirds.

113.

"Everything happens for a reason" is getting a little
too hard to believe in
Because what did I do to deserve this pain, what sin?
I want to go with the divine's plan but I try to find
answers and signs that I'll wake up one day and finally
feel free
As if I truly want what's best in the long run, when I
actually just want you to come running back to me.

114.

You made me afraid to be soft ever again so I hardened faster than I ever did before
Took me so long to put you on that pedestal but it took you two seconds to drop me to the floor
Made me rethink and replay whether any of this was even real
The thought of you playing pretend makes it hard for me to heal
It's not my fault I love this hard and see the gold glimmer in a sea of coal
All I have to show for it is a string of sleepless nights and my sanity that you stole.

115.

You hated the color green
I let it slide because, for the first time in a long time, I felt seen
I told you it was my birthstone and you told me we don't have to like the same things
If it were me I would have made a sweet comment to you, but I told myself relationships are more than preference in potential engagement rings.

116.

They say it's time to grow up now. How can I?
When they say you should have it all figured out by now all I hear is a lie
Panic attacks thinking about uncertainty, well I've had plenty
Going through my angsty teen phase in my twenties
Hoping they can understand just what I'm going through
I'm expected to know it all but I honestly never truly know what to say or do
I wander this big city forgetting that this is something I always wished I had
Maybe a little youth, a little uncertainty during this time of my life isn't so bad.

117.

You kissed my hands leaving bruises that eventually turned to scars
Who knew you'd leave before they healed, that we wouldn't even make it that far
Took me months to come to terms with those sweet lies
To realize I comforted you through your lows, feeling like I had to earn your highs
You left glimmers of hope scattered like constellations in the night
I'll look up at them until someone eventually comes and turns on the light.

118.

Sometimes the least amount of words speaks the loudest
Sometimes the most educated people can be the proudest
Because what we see superficially is rarely the case
The truth is usually cloaked in a veil and hard to trace
Society has made us think that what we aren't is what we need to be
And creating a persona for others will set us free
From the judging eyes glaring from all sides
Destroying creativity and creating divides.

119.

Losing you was hard, but realizing how quickly I lost myself when loving you was harder
I didn't realize that holding you close would push me farther and farther
You consumed me while dimming my light till there was nothing but darkness
I ran from my inner wounds into your arms not realizing the starkness
Between true love and this lingering loss
Because love isn't supposed to come at such a cost
It's supposed to comfort you while respecting your autonomy
Instead you effortlessly tore my soul apart, tarnishing every part of me.

120.

When my time comes and my eyes close for the very last time
Please don't mourn my loss as if someone has committed a crime
This is merely the natural order telling me my purpose was fulfilled
My impact was made, there was nothing left for me to build
My soul was ripe for the heavens, if it stayed any longer it might spoil
My body was molded with clay and longed to once again merge with the soil
So when you feel as though I will not hear you when you scream, no matter how loud
Just know I will always be near, in the silver lining of the cloud.

121.

I see you happy with her, I see the way you stare
I see the love in your eyes, I see you caress her hair
As if I was never your guiding light, your North Star
My body bled your favorite colors, I wonder if it'll ever scar
You made it a point to claim me as your territory, leave your mark
Why don't you tell her I showed you that part of Central Park?
God knows I should forget, I deserve better than this pain of the past
But what if this wasn't only my first love, but also my last?

122.

I would like to believe you see me as developed film
A soft visual over layed in a warm orange hue,
reminding you of simpler times
Not the high definition technology capturing all my
insecurities
I want to be remembered as that slightly blurred
image that reminds you of home
Not a replica of the reality you so desperately want to
escape.

123.

This loneliness creeps in the moment you leave
It suffocates me slowly making it hard to breath
I feel the weight of my own existence
You were always my distraction, I can't handle this distance
I lie to you daily, reassuring you I'm doing just fine
But I'm falling apart at the seams, losing this little mind of mine.

124.

I got everything I wanted, or at least that was what I thought
Was all the pain and suffering worth this education I bought?
I achieved the success they sold to me wrapped in a pretty bow
Is a piece of paper and intense anxiety all I have to show?
I started hating on others for doing too much
Maybe because I was just jealous that they didn't give a fuck
They didn't care what others thought but im crippled by their gaze
I guess this uncertainty doesn't ever leave you, it stays.

125.

Her kindness was mistaken for security and no one ever knew
That she was completely broken inside never knowing what to do
She didn't want to ask for help because she felt like a burden
Was she being dramatic or ungrateful for feeling this way? She could never be certain.
So she bottled it up inside until no one could ever tell
That she was ready to burst at the seams living through

126.

You always leaned on me till you found the strength to push me away
I hadn't felt love like this before so in your rejection I always heard a "stay"
I finally cut the cord on this unfair love affair, people tell me I'm free
But I still find myself skipping over songs because it's too painful to have my reality sung back to me.

127.

I always waited for the this day, I always wanted to be here
I always thought the pieces would fall into place with nothing to fear
But now I'm on the other side wondering if this journey was even worth the pain
I go through the motions appeasing the crowd, was all of this in vain?
I've been living for the show of it all, but I rarely feel alive
Is this what it feels like to be 25?

128.

Do you think about me anymore?
Or is it as easy to forget me as when you walked out
that door
I'm sure your new girl is softer than me, more
palatable to your lifestyle
She'll meet your family in November and in May she'll
be walking down that aisle
I keep thinking, "Was I too loud? Did I come on too
strong?"
But since when was innocent passion so wrong?
I wonder if this lingering sadness I feel follows you
with everything you do
I wonder if the painful reminder of us will soon be
your something blue.

129.

The city lights looked a little blurry with the rain but it felt right
We ran on the slippery pavement as I clutched your trench coat so tight
Did you know that day I decided to let you in?
Did you know that day I decided you were worth the sin?
My soaking wet clothes had your radiator to keep them warm and I had you
I said I could stay in your arms forever and you said you could stay here too
Little did you know those simple words meant so much to me then
Little did I know I could never see the rainy city the same again.

130.

I told myself feeling too much was a sign of weakness
Or maybe I learned that along the way, I blame my meekness
Strength has always been imposed on women as if it defines their worth
They must bear the burdens of this world far beyond giving birth
But you have deprived me of my divine feminine for too long
Watch me take in every moment for myself, relish every song
I'll cry till my cheeks fill out my palms and my eyes turn red
And I won't regret anything I felt, not a single tear I shed.

131.

He haunts me in the cold of the night
Hiding in the corner of my mind away from the light
Vowing not to reveal himself until I finally find a way out
The moment security graces me he returns filling me with doubt.
Sirens learn from him just how to entrance the innocent
I don't think he will stop till he is conquered by his equivalent
Someone equally as lethal, equally as horrid
A villain masked in beauty, leaving his soul torrid.

132.

I isolate myself when my surroundings become too much
I sink into the comfort of this darkness that's both cold and comforting to the touch
It's becoming harder and harder to see the light, to see the sublime
I overexpose my photos to find brightness in this dull life
It's not that no one is here for me, or I was left here alone
I just can't hear their empty advices and their condescending tone
They'll never know what I'm going through, they'll never know how to empathize
So I'll continue to lament in private, slowly closing my eyes.

133.

Every day she woke up from bed playing a character
She'd go downstairs with a fake smile no one suspected her
Walking into school with false confidence was second nature by now
This is what you do in a place like this, you blend in with the high brow
She was so naive, this painful existence was the only life she new
Until she realized it wasn't supposed to be this way, all the suffering she went through
So she escaped into the night taking nothing but a duffle and what was left of her soul
Picking up the pieces they robbed of her, making herself once again whole
Years go by, and one day she looked in the mirror and facing her reflection was no longer a chore
Yet she knows the masses continue to say she looked so much better before.

134.

I gave you so much grace why don't I get the same?
For all of your inevitable failures, why was I really to blame?
Been the punching bag for so many people I've been left forever sore
Never expected anyone to stay, but a part of me dies every time they walk out that door
I thought you might be different so I took the time to piece you back together
Just for you to need space and end up giving her your always and forever.

135.

Wish I would have cried back then, maybe I wouldn't
be so numb today
Wish I would have let myself feel it all when you
decided not to stay
For the sake of strength I wept in silence, not making
a sound
Till I became unrecognizable to the people who
actually stuck around.

136.

Looking at beautiful photos of myself till I deconstruct
them into something unsightly
I throw my phone across the room and hold onto my
cold covers so tightly
How could God do this to me? Was I not worth a more
beautiful form?
I've been branded as the optimist, so I paint on my
smile ready to perform
You see a shining mirrorball brightening the room
I see a premature flower refusing to bloom
When will it be my turn to feel effortless and free?
Maybe I have another year, maybe two, maybe three

137.

Was I ever your North Star or just an asteroid on the outskirts of your orbit?
Did my rays brighten your path or deter from it?
You never really told me where you wanted to end up
I never let your secrets bother me, kept my half full cup
Because you told me I was the constant in your uncharted dream
Until one day you decided there was no need for the way I beam
So you stranded me in this nothingness, not leaving trace
Broke me to my core all in the name of space.

138.

We don't really talk anymore and I guess I got what I wanted
I prayed for you to forget about me because your memory left me haunted
But when I heard about your life for the first time from the lens of another I felt a pit inside me
Because I'm no longer your first call, is this loneliness or feeling free?

139.

Applaud yourself for the little things
For waking up in the morning, making your bed,
brewing a coffee, leaving your apartment
These moves can feel heavier when the weight of the
world becomes too much
Don't let anyone tell you, you were lazy today, or you
could have done more
Because you did your best and that is more than
enough.

140.

It's so much easier to not feel it
It's so much simpler to say it's not a right fit
Running from love is a hobby of mine, I try to not get too attached
I don't want to be a pawn in a complicated plan he's hatched
Because I fall deeper, and he thinks "leave her," and I'll be too broken to put up a fight
So I wonder if it's better to just rock myself to sleep at night.

141.

Poets are said to be idealists
Romantics who avoid reality
What if I told you we uncover the realest parts of you?
What if I told you we're brave enough to face the
truths you hide from in the name of reason?
We look darkness in the eye and describe it with such
beauty even the beast couldn't tell the difference.

Mariam Shams Tabrez

142.

This sadness in me consumes the lightest parts of my mind
How can I control the thought that sanity is something I'll never find
It's taken half of my body, lightening the load from the bed in which it lies
It's hollowed out my cheeks and made lifeless these once glimmering eyes
But all they see is I've changed, matured, grown into my features
I guess this is the natural order and after all, humans are habitual creatures.

143.

Thought you hated on me for no reason
Turns out we're the same life living in different seasons
Felt like I could never do anything right and I'd always be a disgrace
Who knew I was just the mirror image of your face?
We've lived the same life so I'm just asking for some understanding
Because you know this burden is much heavier than it looks from where you're standing.

144.

I don't hold a grudge for me, I hold a grudge for her
For her this is all a little to real, for me it's now just a blur
I've licked my wounds till they healed, she's been newly severed
For me seeing you happy brings me joy, for her seeing you move on is the hardest endeavor
She's smiling through the bleeding, I'm expressing myself in the most honest way
She can't hide from your betrayal, I choose my peace over the painful stay
She sometimes visits me in the deepest parts of night and reminds me of you
I hold her tightly and tell her the story of how much she grew.

145.

How could he love every part of who I am when we
meet over a blue screen?
How could I know him if we never discussed our
hopes and dreams?
First meeting in a crowded room filled with
judgmental eyes
Where we put our best selves forward and tell well-
rehearsed lies
Instead of sharing the deepest parts of who we are
under the city lights
I want the wonderful complexity, I want the uncertain,
I want the inevitable fights
Not some manufactured connection made by those
with good intentions
That results in a loveless marriage with value only in
our pensions.

146.

Something is shifting
I can't quite grasp what it is, maybe the tides, the stars,
the planets, maybe it's me
I feel this sense of calm yet unsettling anticipation for
what hasn't even entered my life yet
As though I can feel my old self waving me goodbye
and a new version of me entering this new phase
I'm scared to let her go, she held me down for so long
But I know she's proud of where I am now and for that
I am blessed.

147.

I wish someone would have told me
That complicated isn't what I thought it would be
It isn't an undying fire that can't be described in words
We weren't two damned lovers shielding ourselves
from the swords
I was holding up our alliance with all my strength
I played the part, I painted a smile on my face, oh I
wish you knew the lengths
That I went to for your companionship, a bond I
thought would last me a lifetime
Only for you to not realize that loving me didn't even
cost a dime
You turned out to be a traitor, the adversary I thought
we would fight together hand in hand
I guess this was some sick jest from the universe, but
I'm still waiting for the joke to land
Because I thought "hard to describe" meant our
connection was unworldly, written in the stars
Not a betrayal so deep it left everlasting scars.

148.

Once so close, the daily motions were taken for granted
Now you say thank you and goodbye as if formalities were always between us
I crave the apathy, the casualness we shared when we were always together
These overt expressions of affection and yearning are building boundaries between us only I seem to see
These utterances signal our separation, signal these good times will soon come to an end
I forever wish for melancholy unity instead.

149.

You're the one I want to spend my life with, I just have this feeling
That you were sent to this earth for me but the thought overwhelms me, sends me reeling
Because I'm afraid to even write this out because I've been so terribly wrong before
And yes I've grown and moved on but those scars left me a little sore
I'm afraid to make you a protagonist in the fantasies that help me sleep
I might build you up and blind myself of reality, I might preemptively leap
Into your arms with a trust that commits common sense fatality
So I'll hold onto these dreams until they become my reality.

150.

Apathy hurts way more than feeling
Knowing I'm crying on the bathroom floor while you're out there healing
I never expected perfection but then again I never expected betrayal
A type of deception that leaves you stranded, leaves you frail
Recounting every moment, every gesture, every word
I have to guess how you're doing now, rely on what I've heard
Shutting down my feelings with logic only you could understand
Breaking my heart into more pieces than the desert has sand
When did I go from your everyday to someone you once knew?
Who was going to tell me the only way out of this is through?

151.

You define your own path, you're destined for what you can't see
Find solace in the fact that you are right where you're supposed to be.

Milton Keynes UK
Ingram Content Group UK Ltd.
UKHW020319070624
443692UK00012B/224/J